On The F

MW00885382

Dot Markers Activity Book

35 pages of farm-themed illustrations
designed to be colored with dot marker pens

This book belongs to:

Blue Elephant Press

A Message for the Grown Ups

Hello and welcome to the world of Blue Elephant Press. This page gives you an overview of this book, how to use it, and where to find more information.

How to use this book:

In this book, you will find:

- 2 practice pages for your child to practice using their dot markers pens
- 35 illustrations with names and a cute elephant shape
- Trim lines to help with cutting out each page from the book, either before your child starts or after they have finished their masterpiece

This book has been designed to be completed with standard dot markers pens and is ideal for children aged 2 years and above. The elephant shapes are designed to trigger your child's imagination. How about encouraging them to color the elephant as well?

We recommend putting a piece of paper or cardboard beneath the page to avoid bleed-through caused by small hands using lots of pressure. :-) Have fun!

Interested in our free resources?

Check out our homepage to see more books, download our free activity sheets, and read our blog. In our blog, we share parenting tips and craft activity ideas to do with your little ones. Our goal is to help you educate them in a fun and creative way.

www.blueelephantpress.com

Explore more of our books!

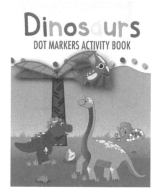

SCAN ME TO GET FREE RESOURCES

SCAN ME TO SEE ALL BOOKS

If you live outside the US, see the last page for the QR code of your country.

Dot Markers Practice Page 1

Practice with your dot markers on this page to perfect your skills!

Dot Markers Practice Page 2

Practice with your dot markers on this page to
perfect your skills!

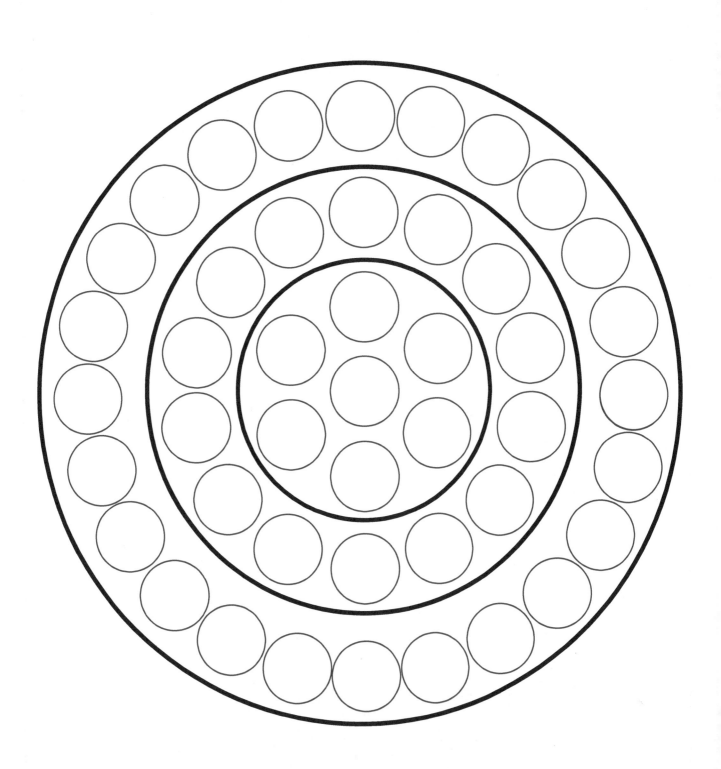

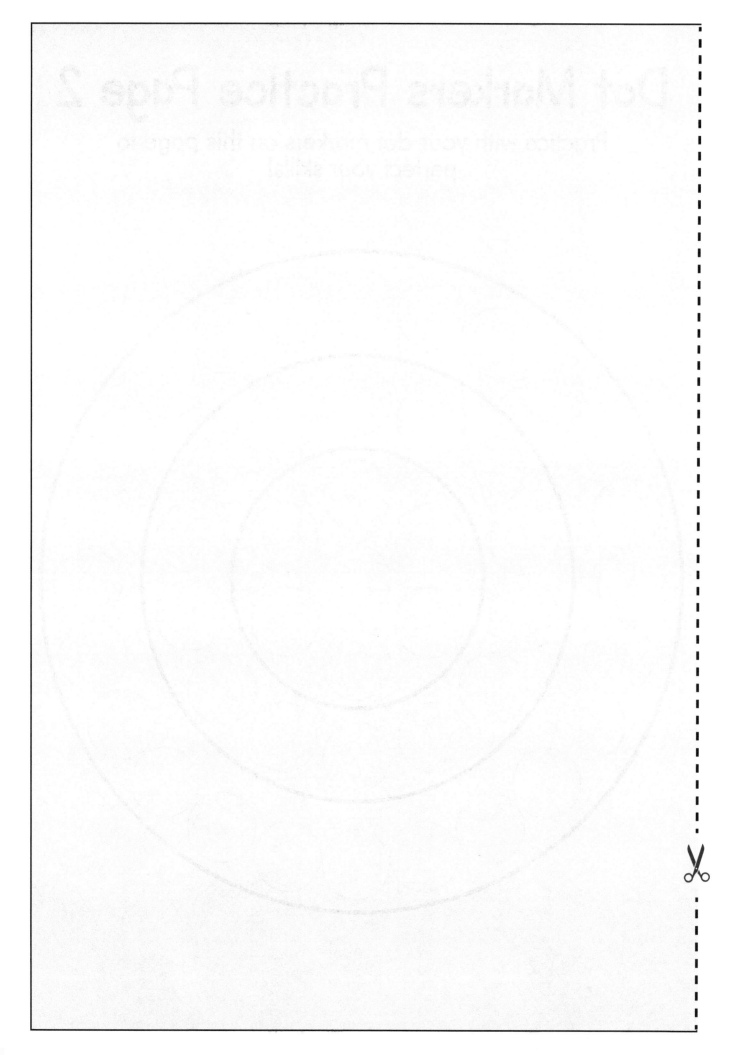

Baby Cow

Happy Horse

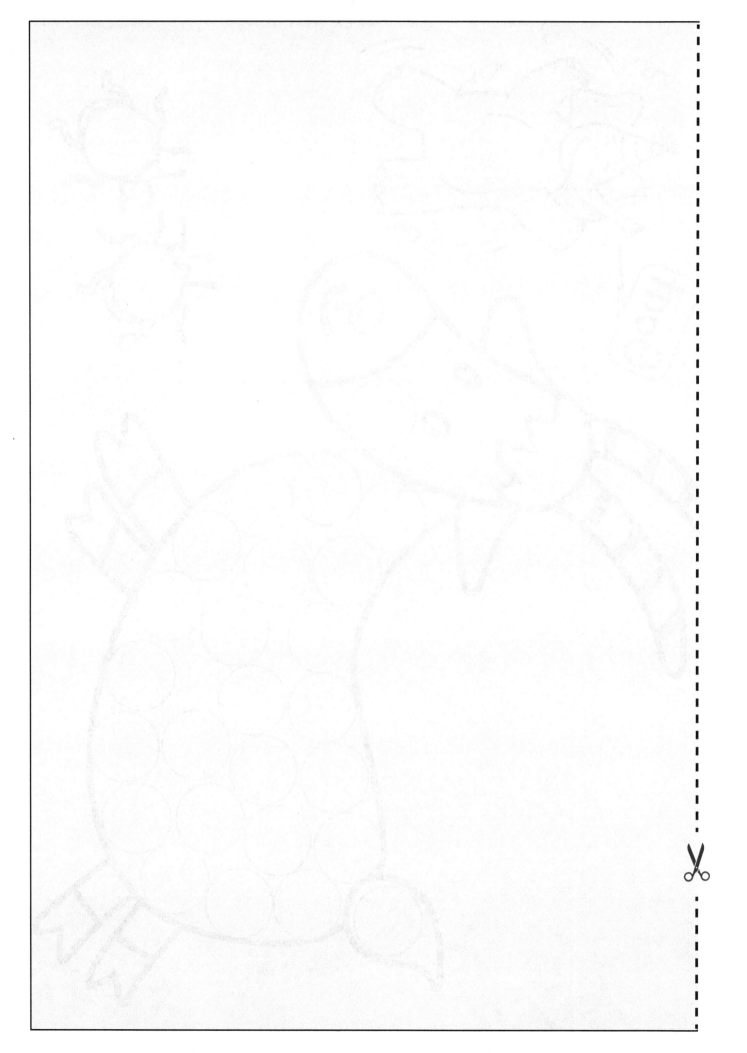

Laughing Rooster

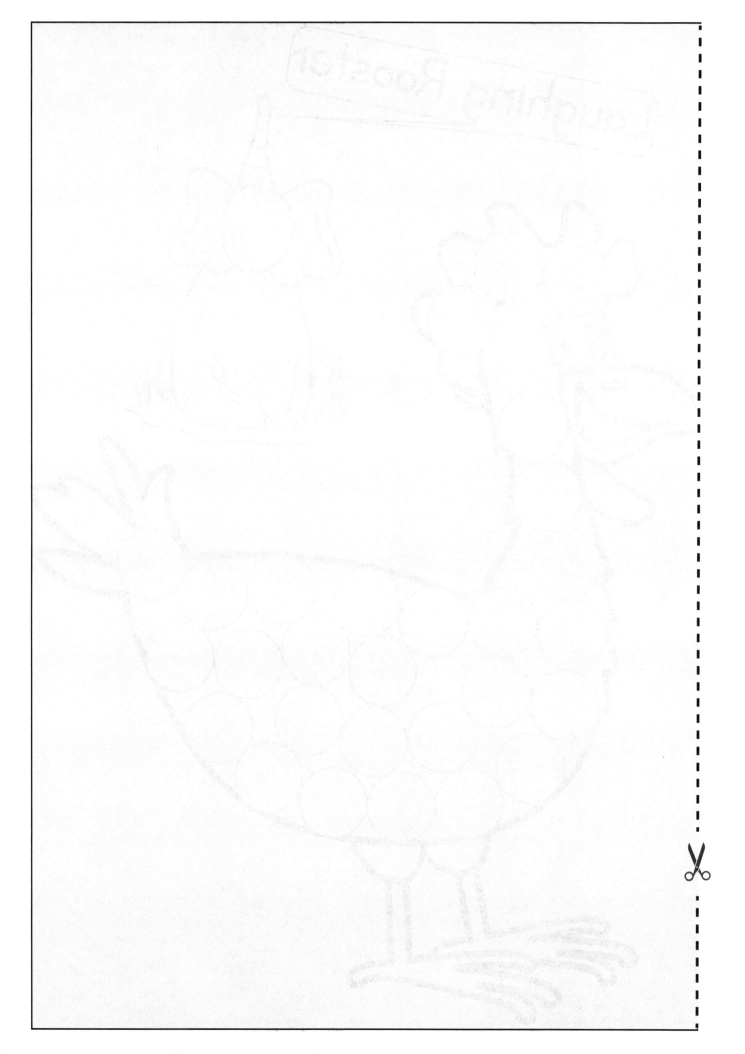

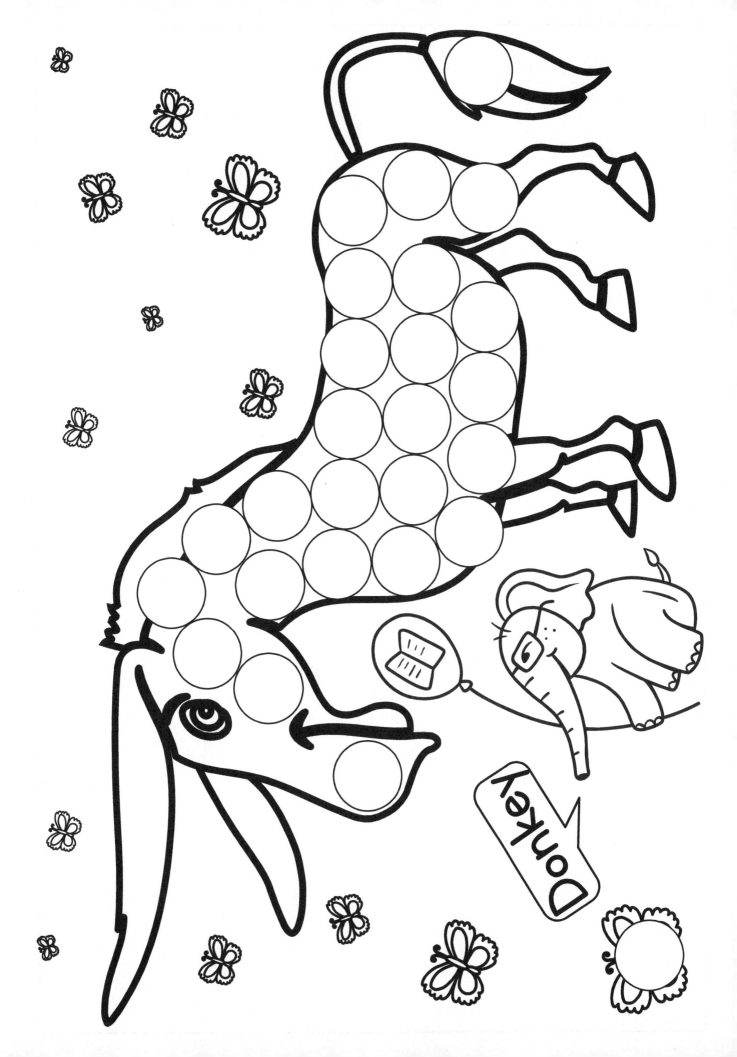

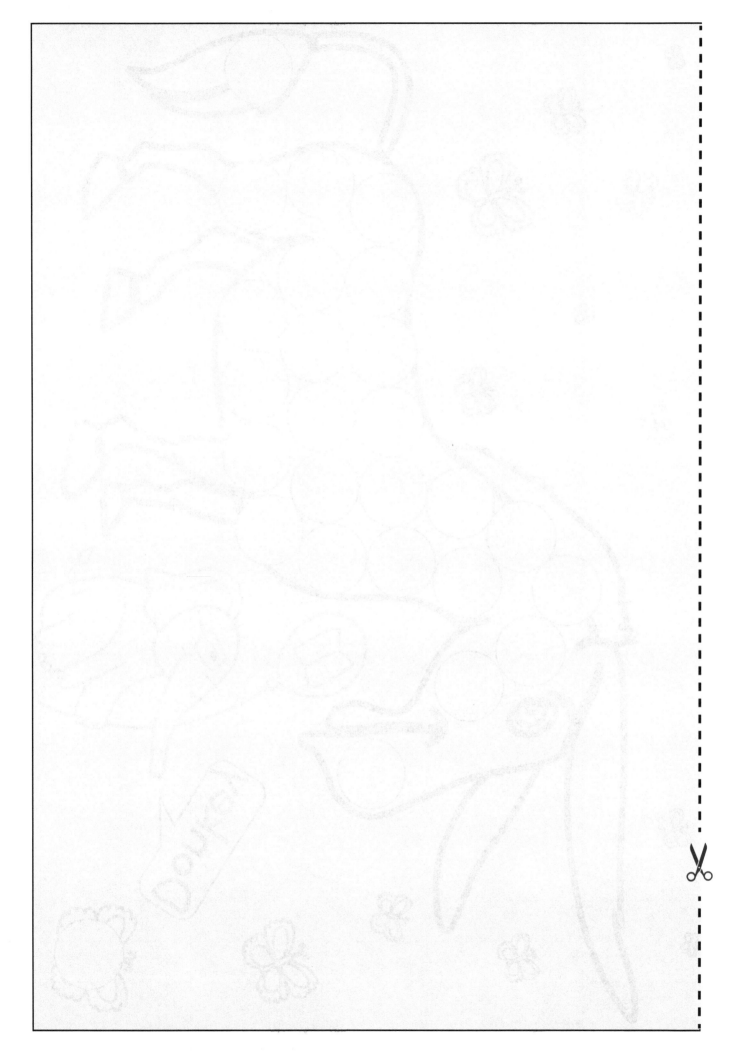

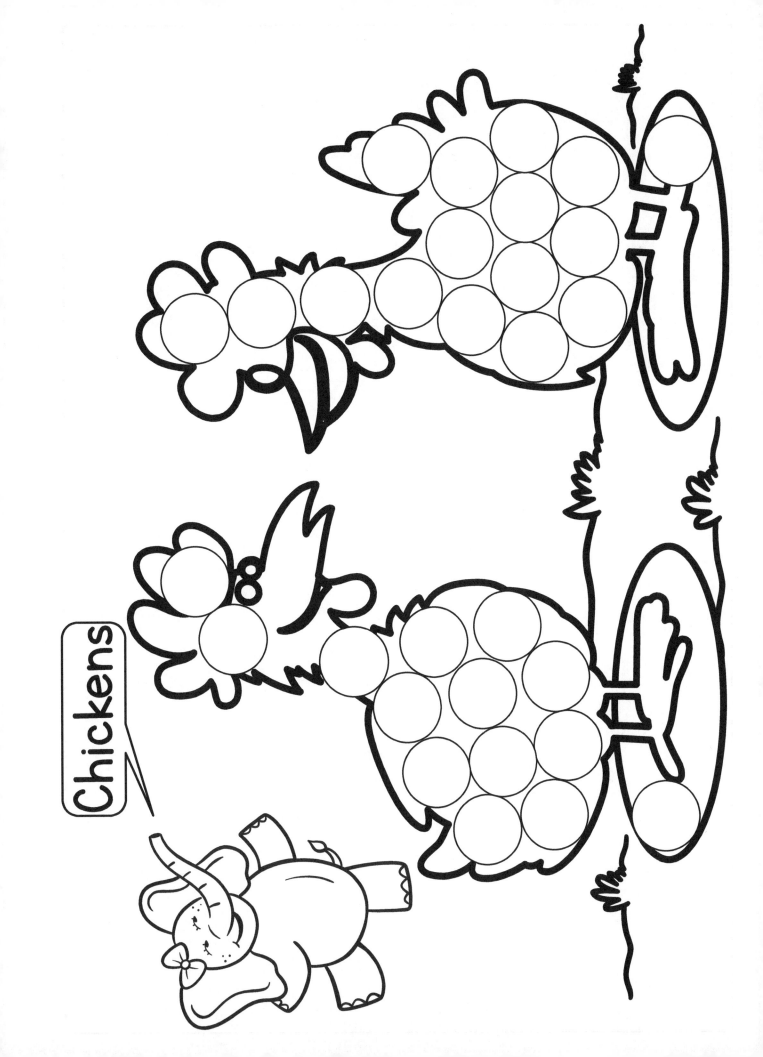

Chickens

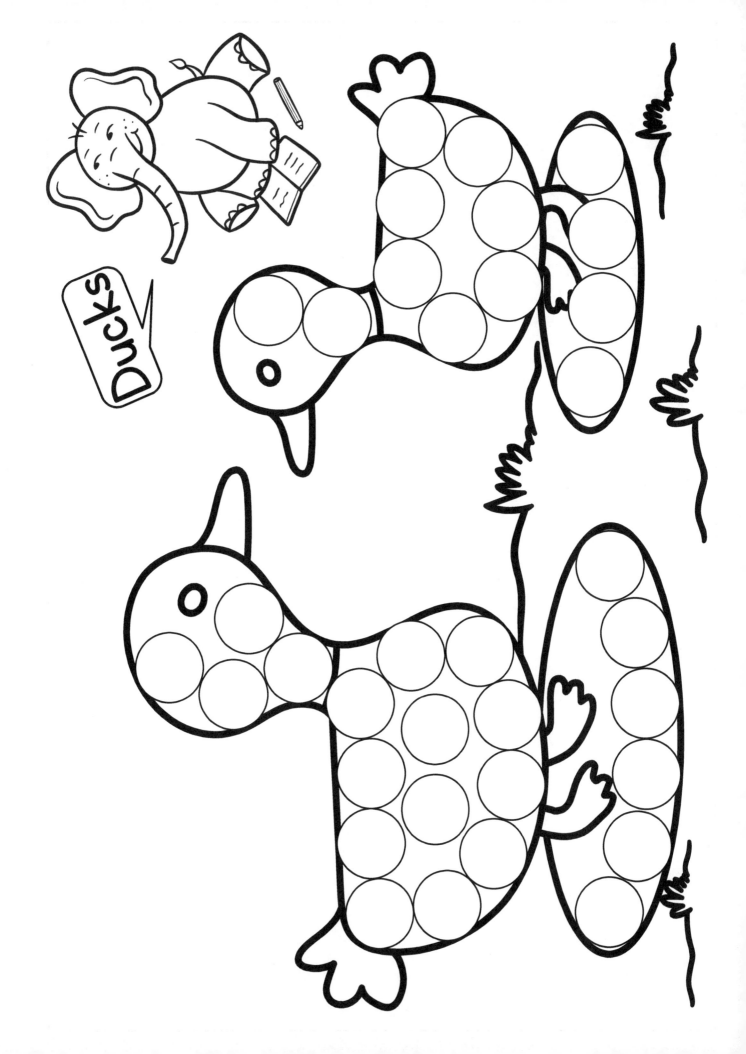

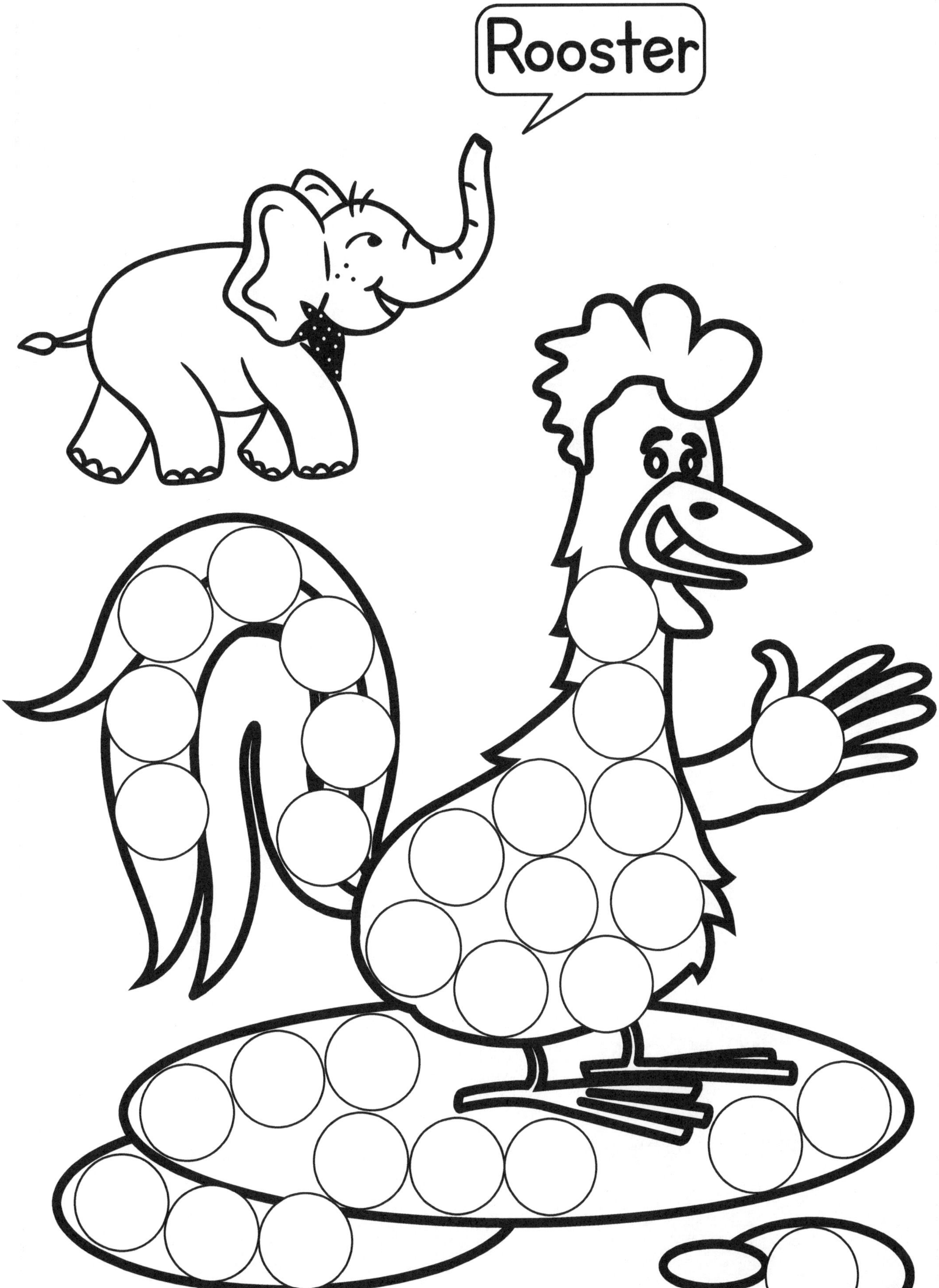
Rooster

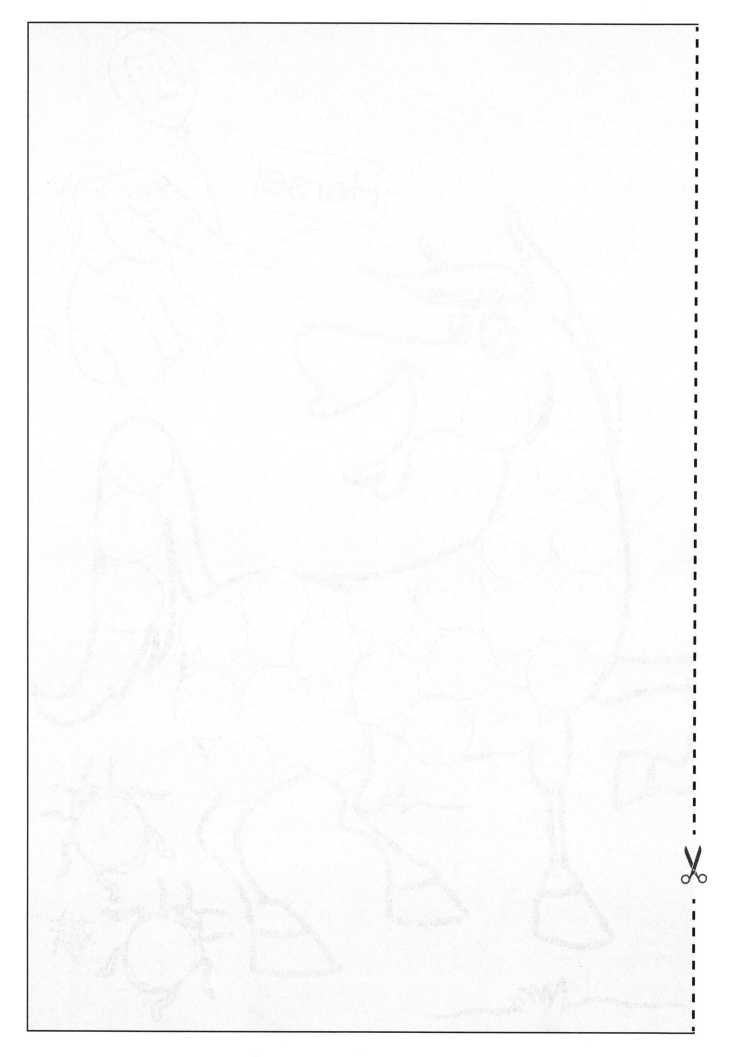

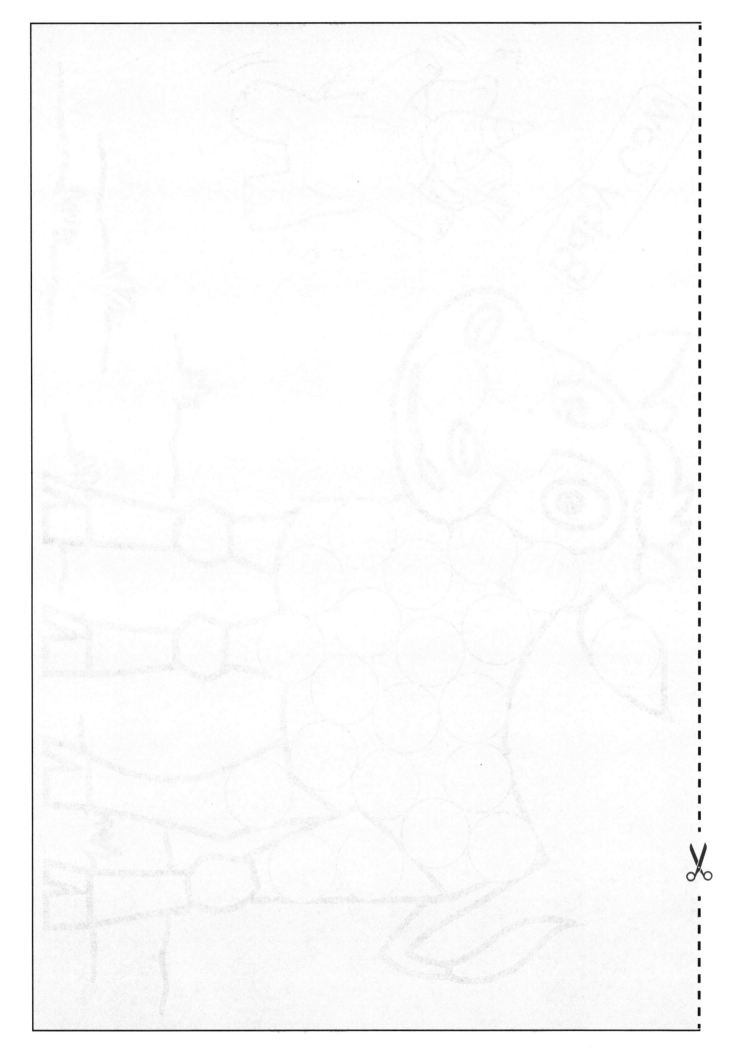

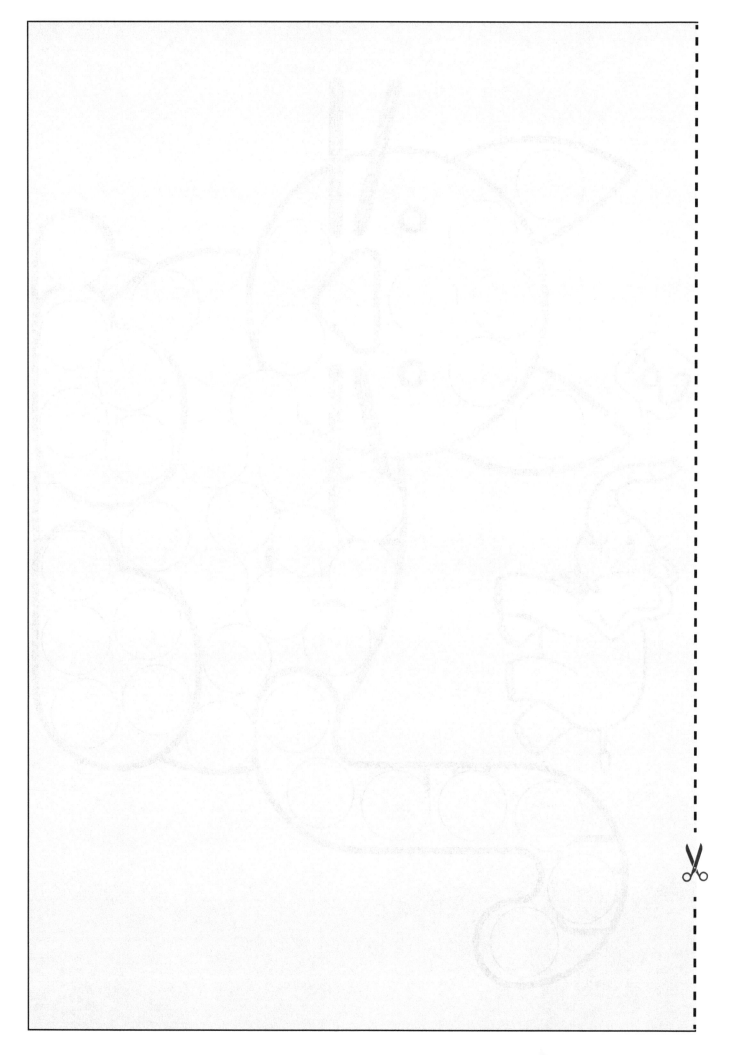

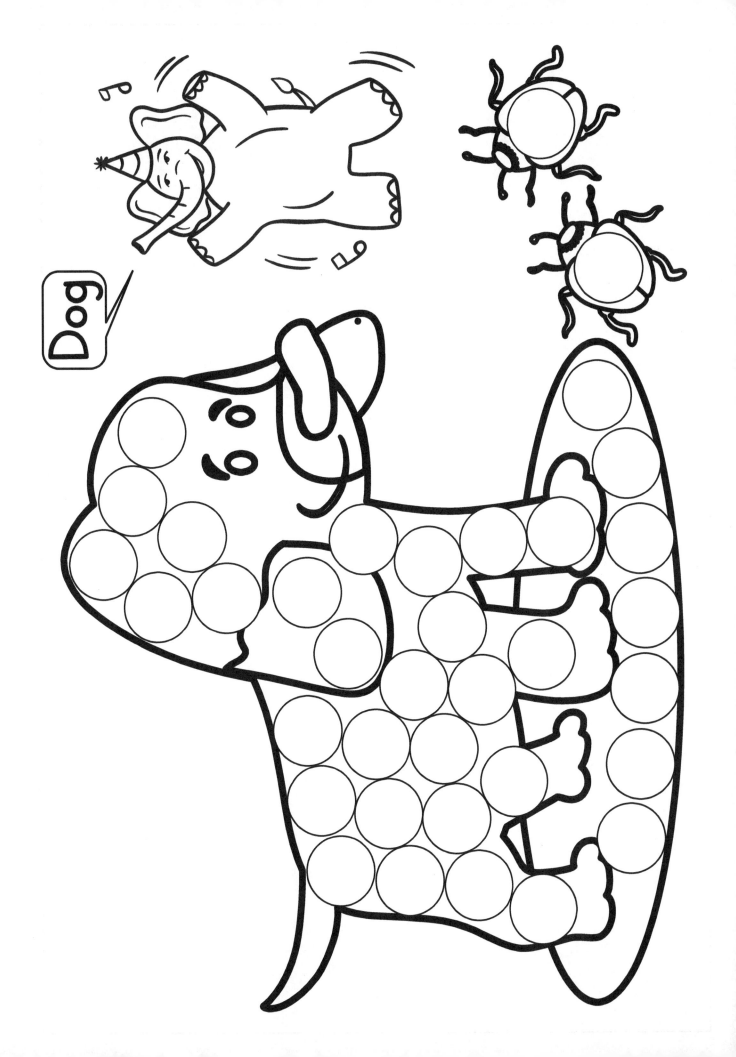

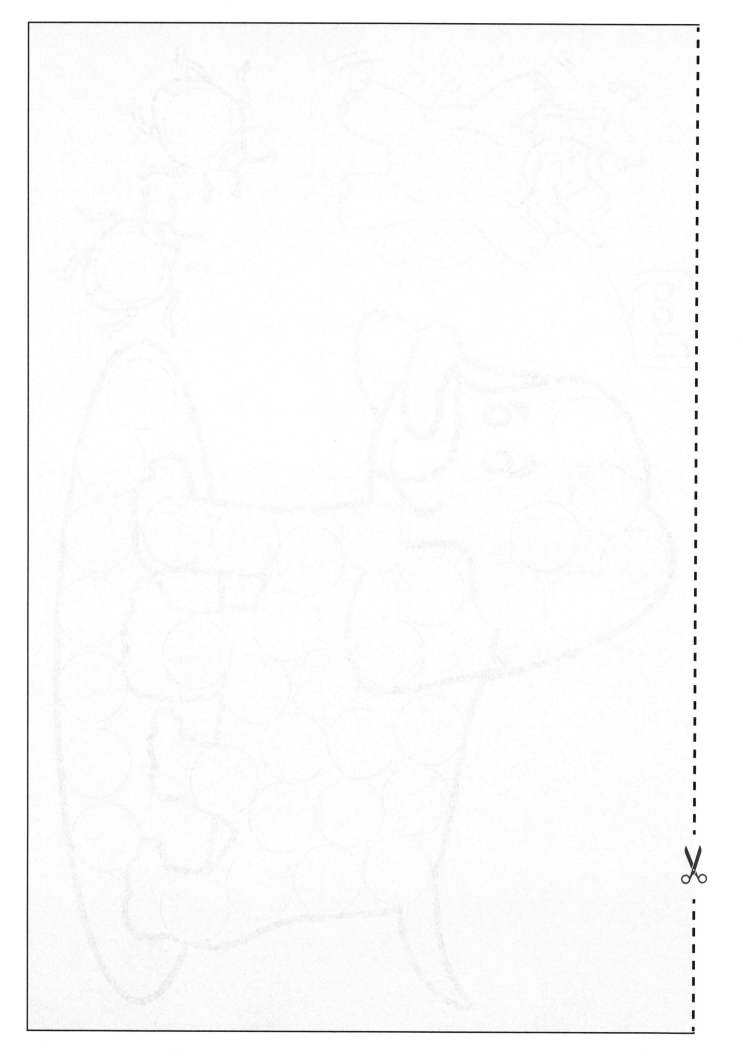

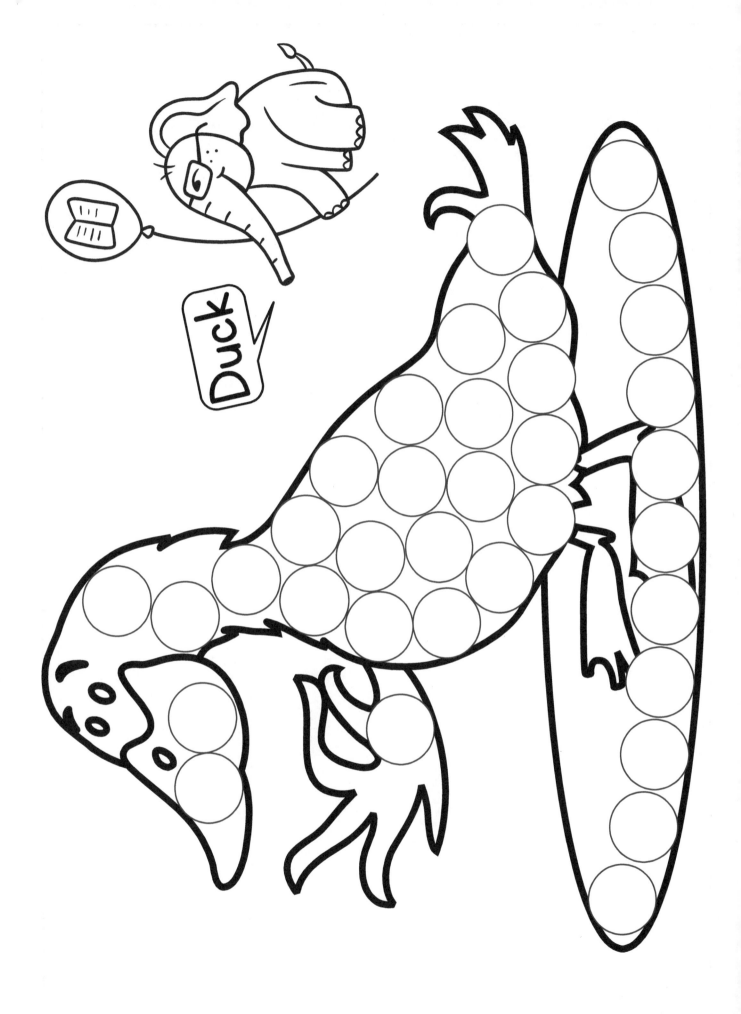

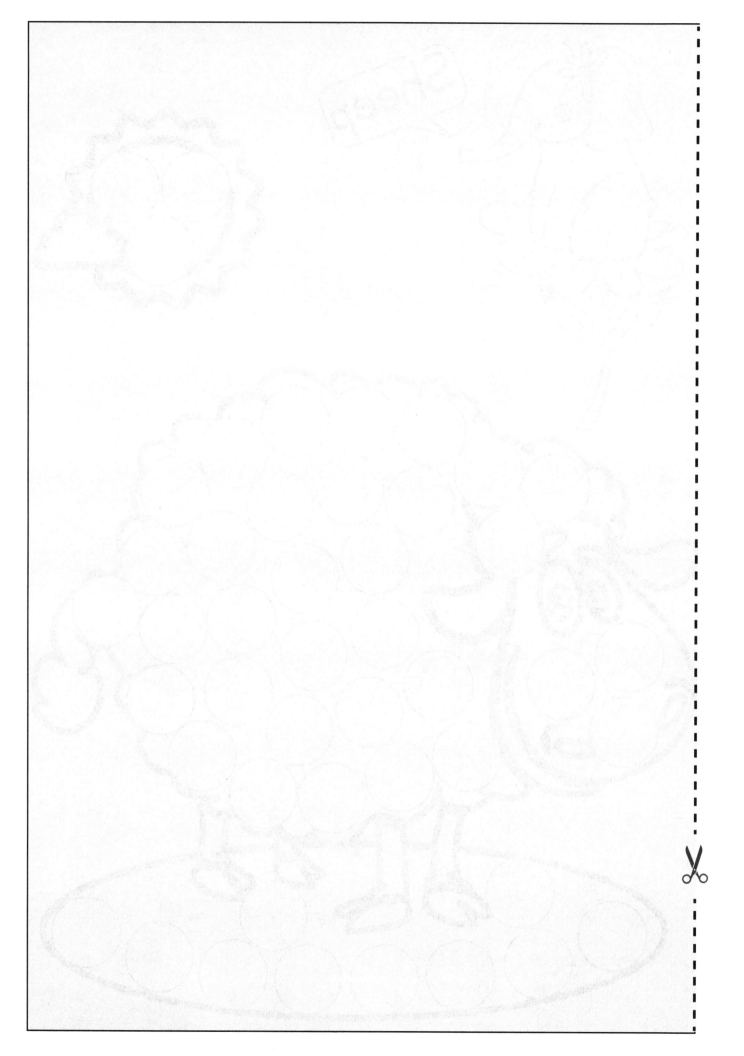

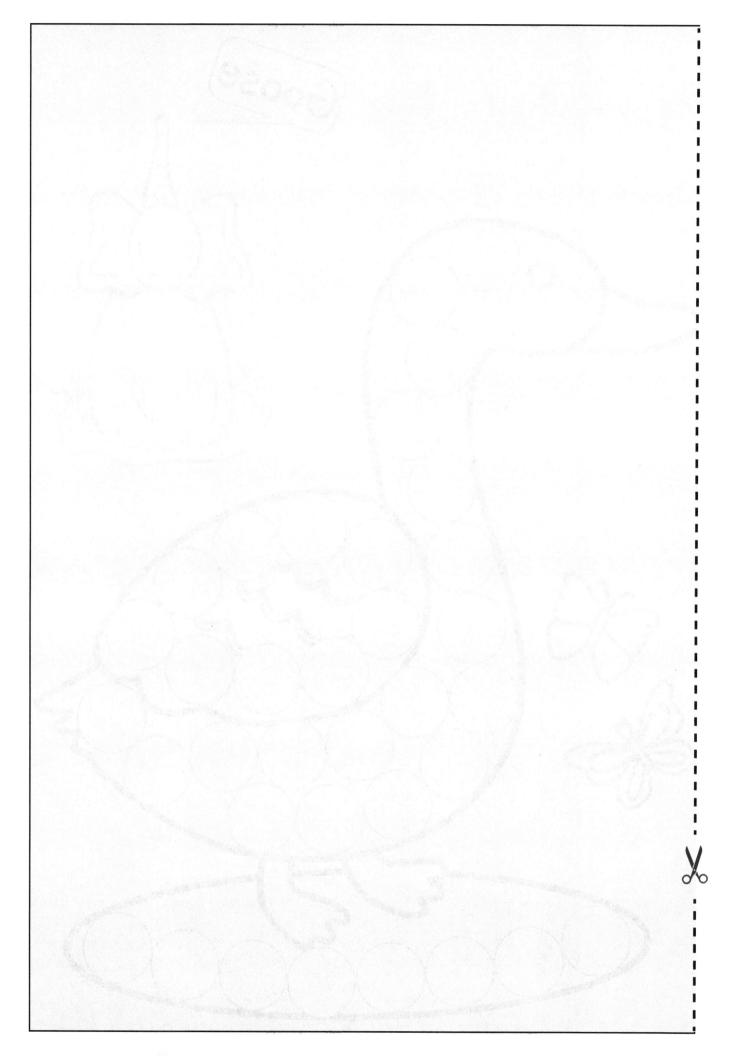

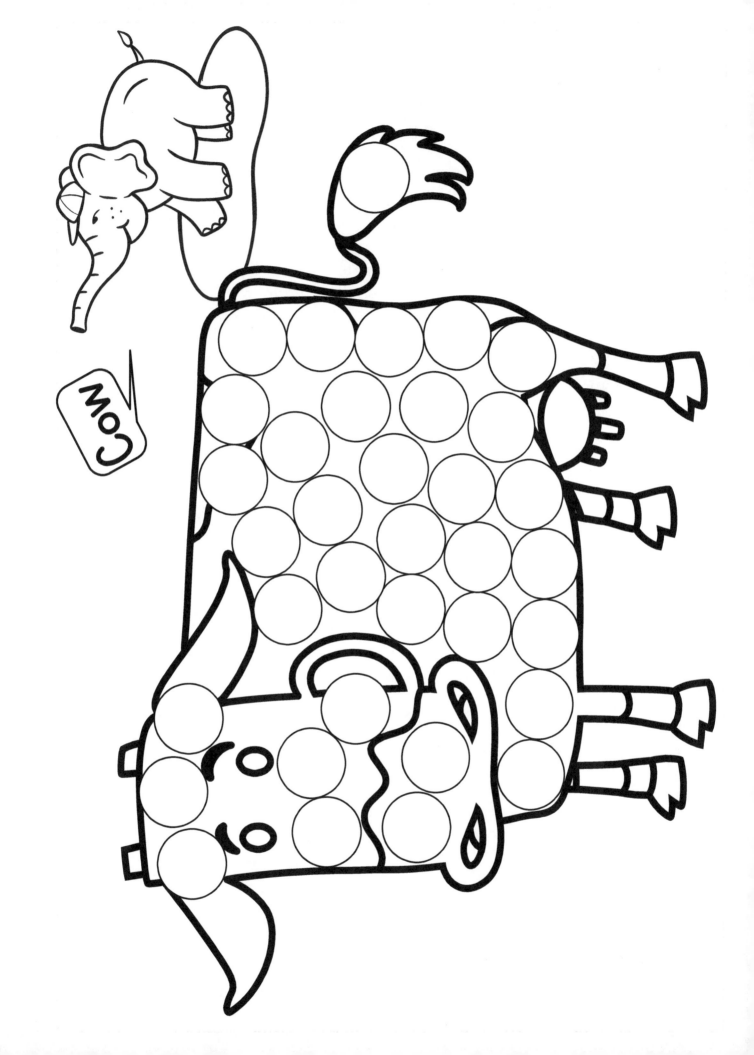

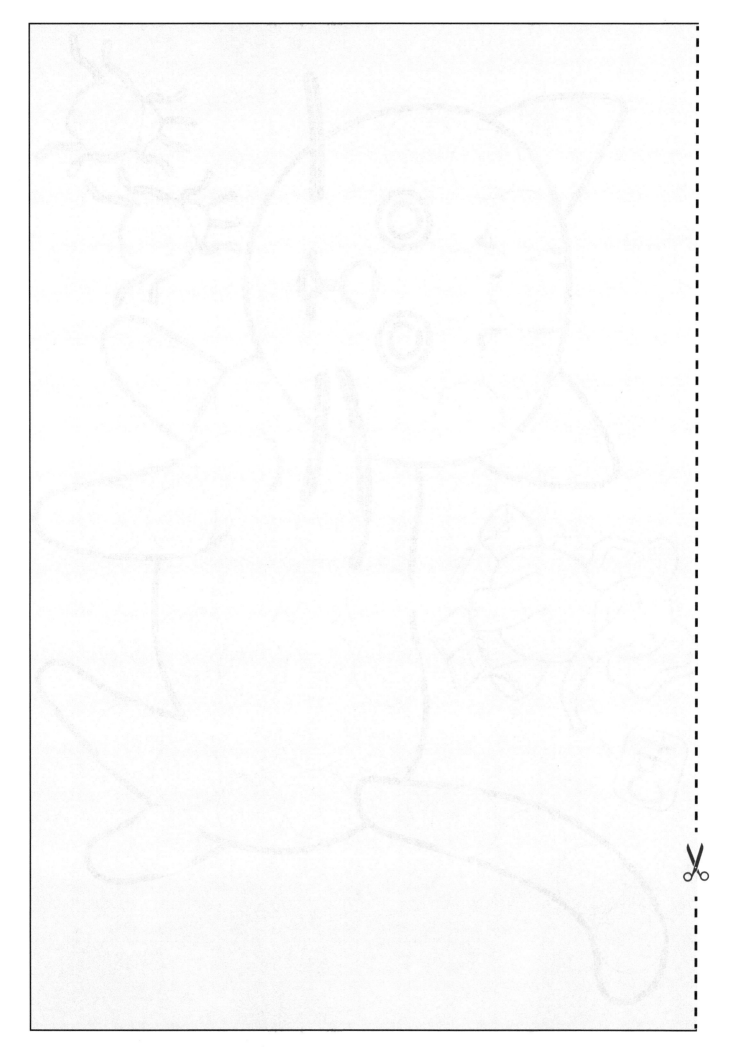

Smiling Ram

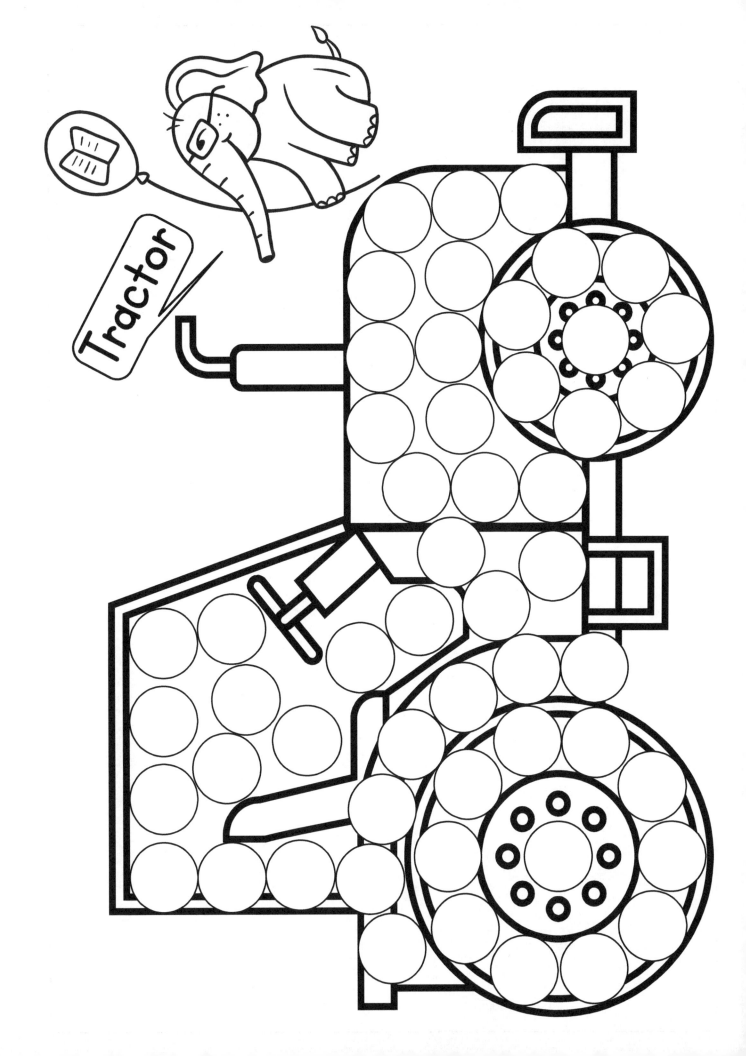

Tractor

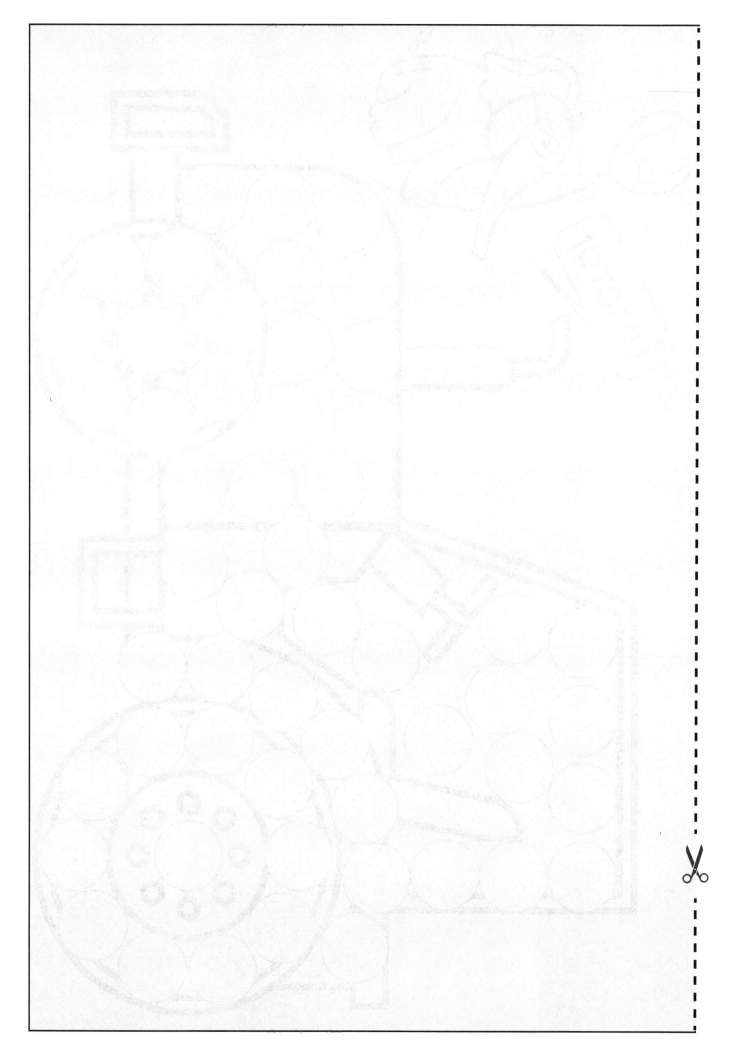

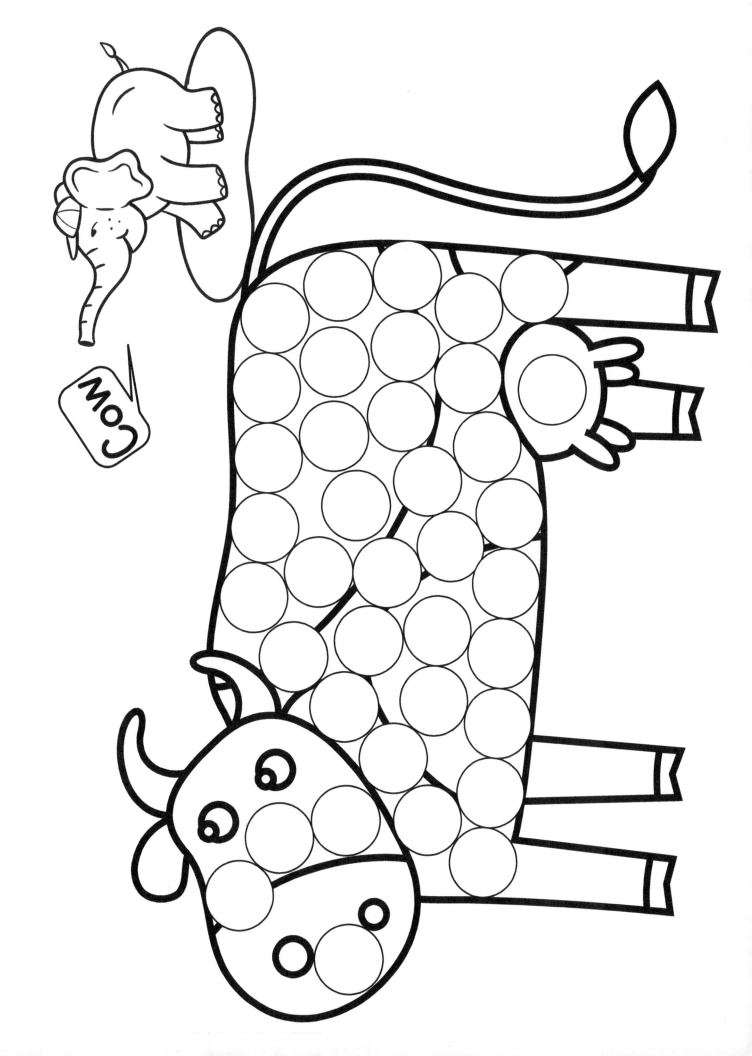

Cow

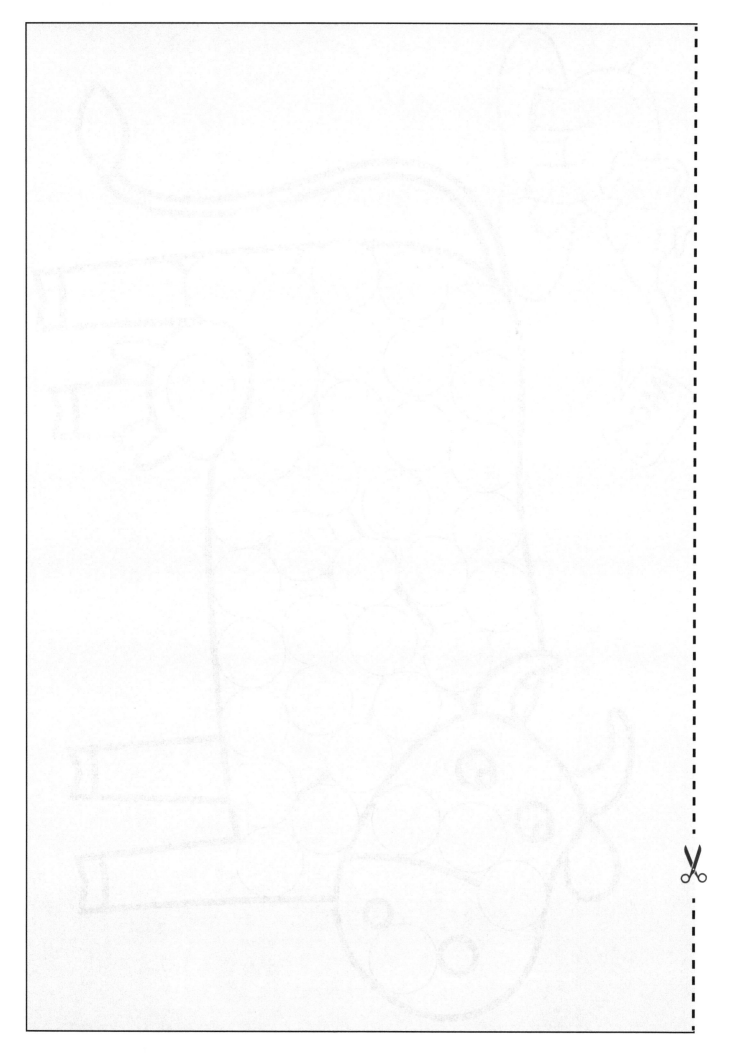

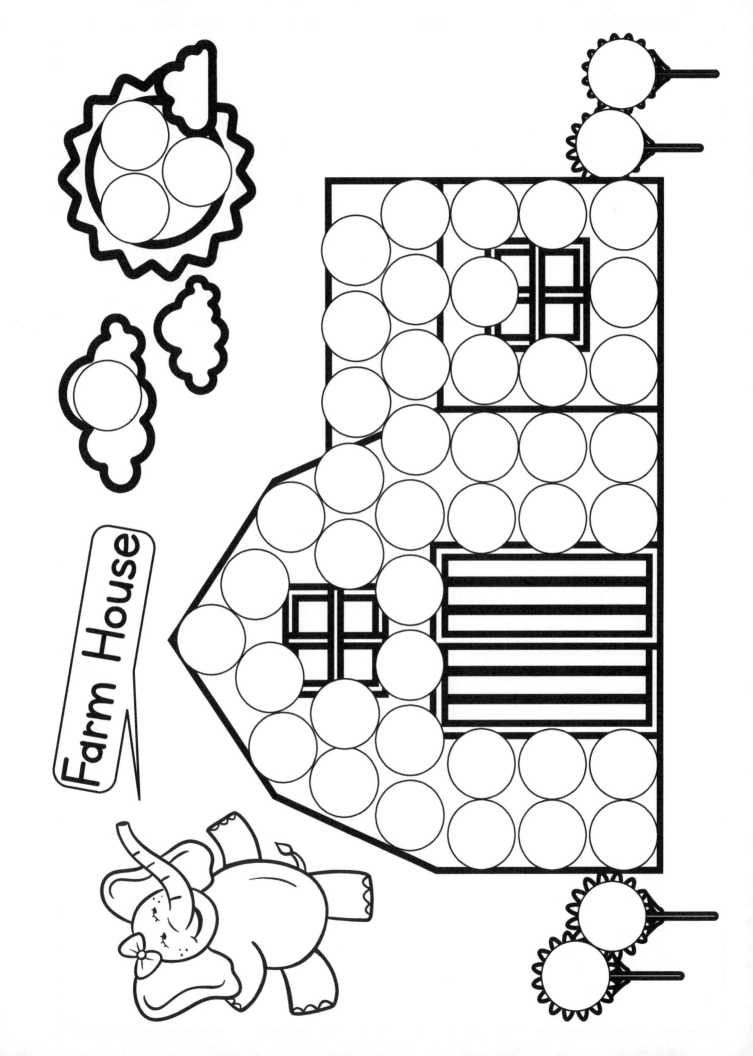

Farm House

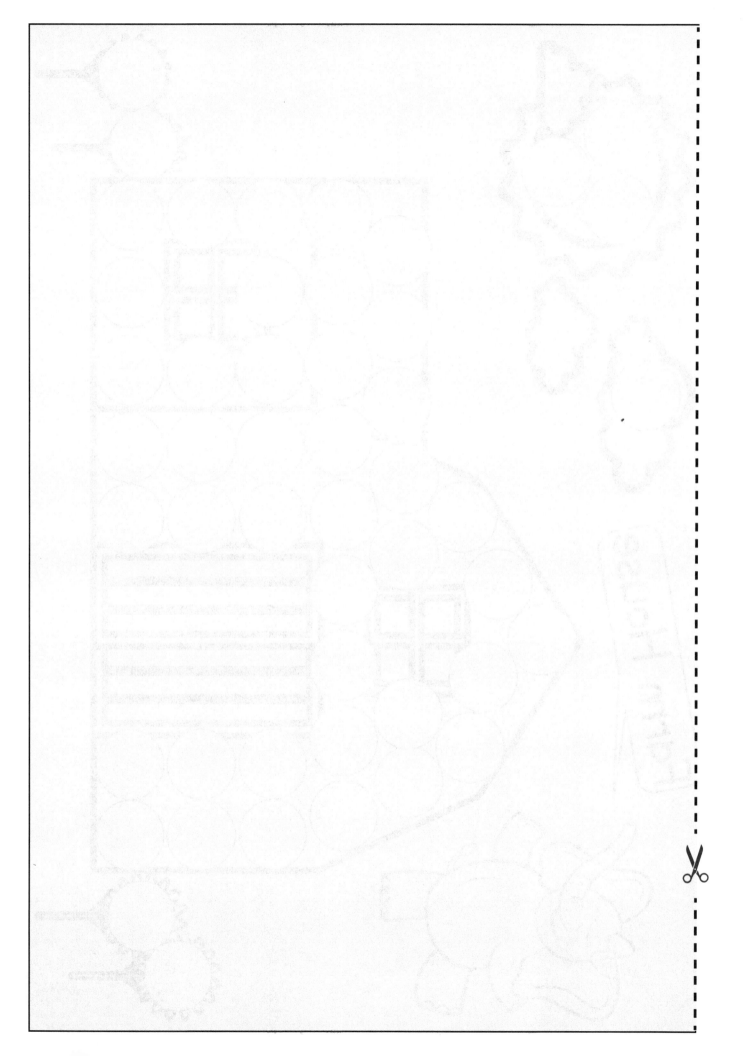

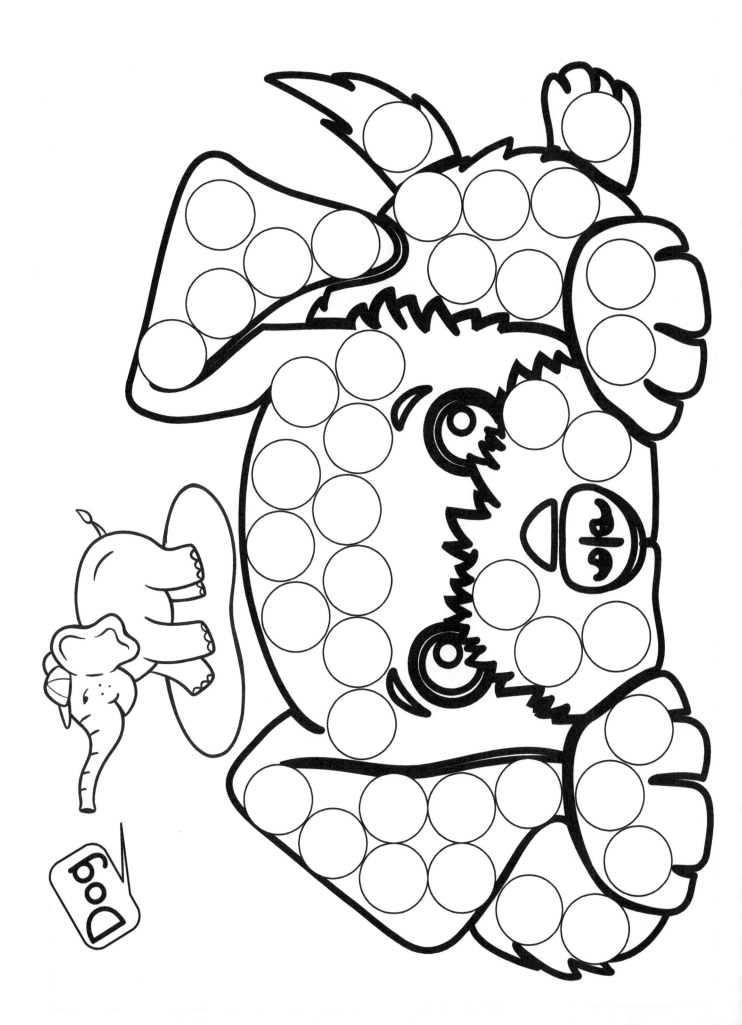

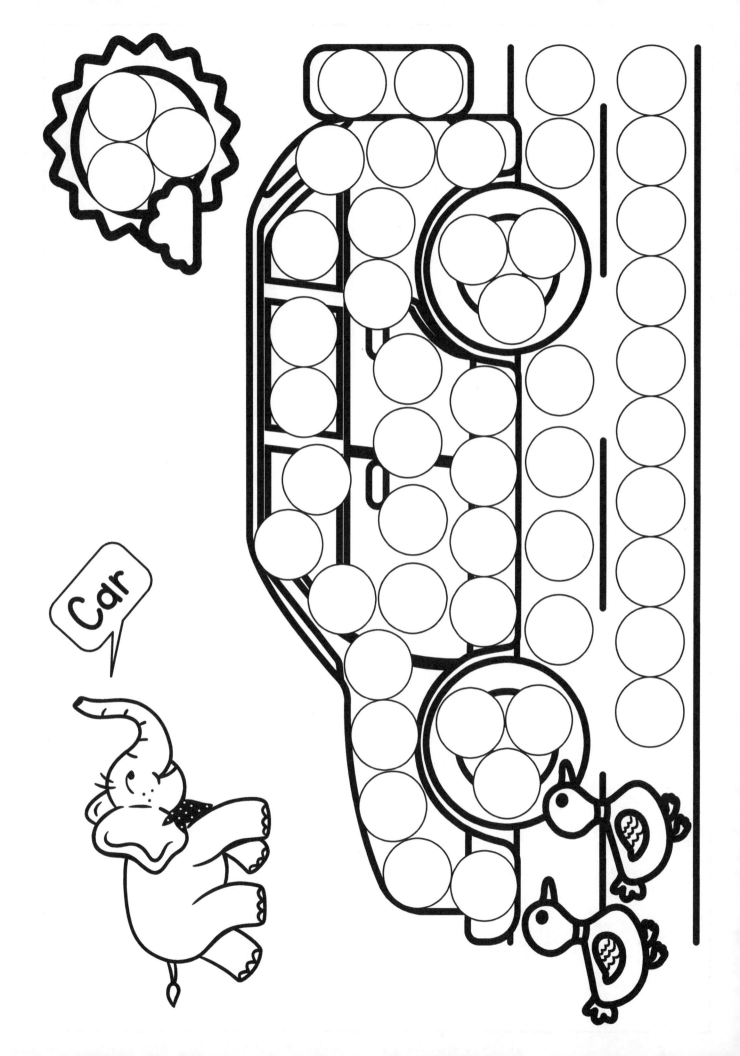

Car

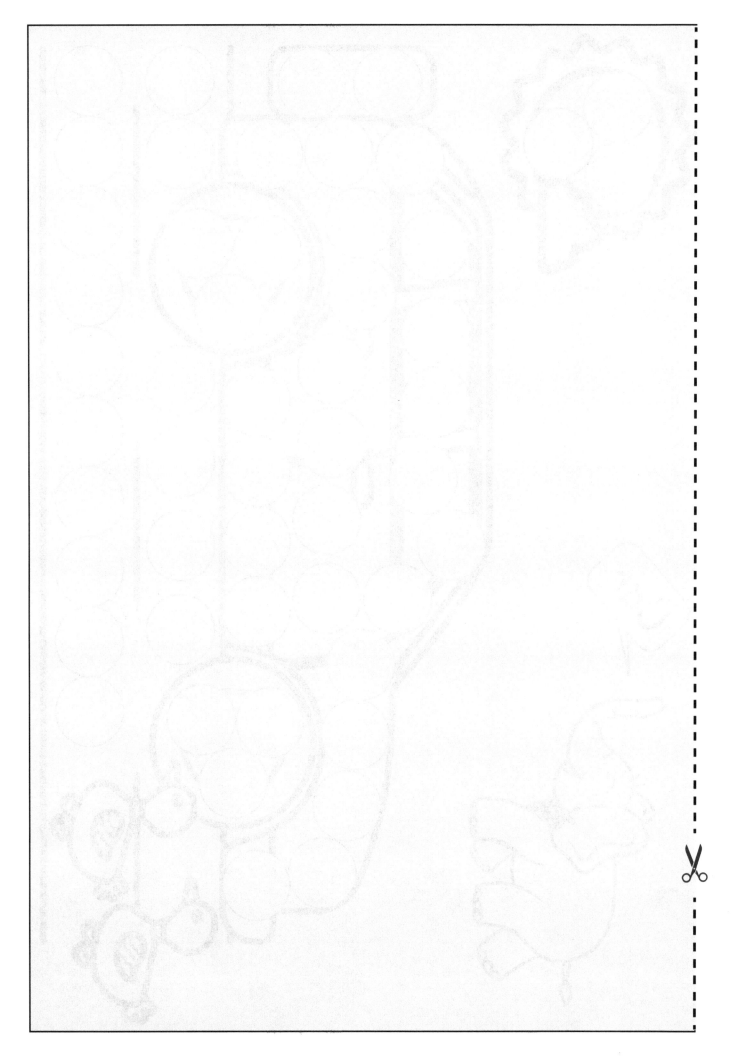

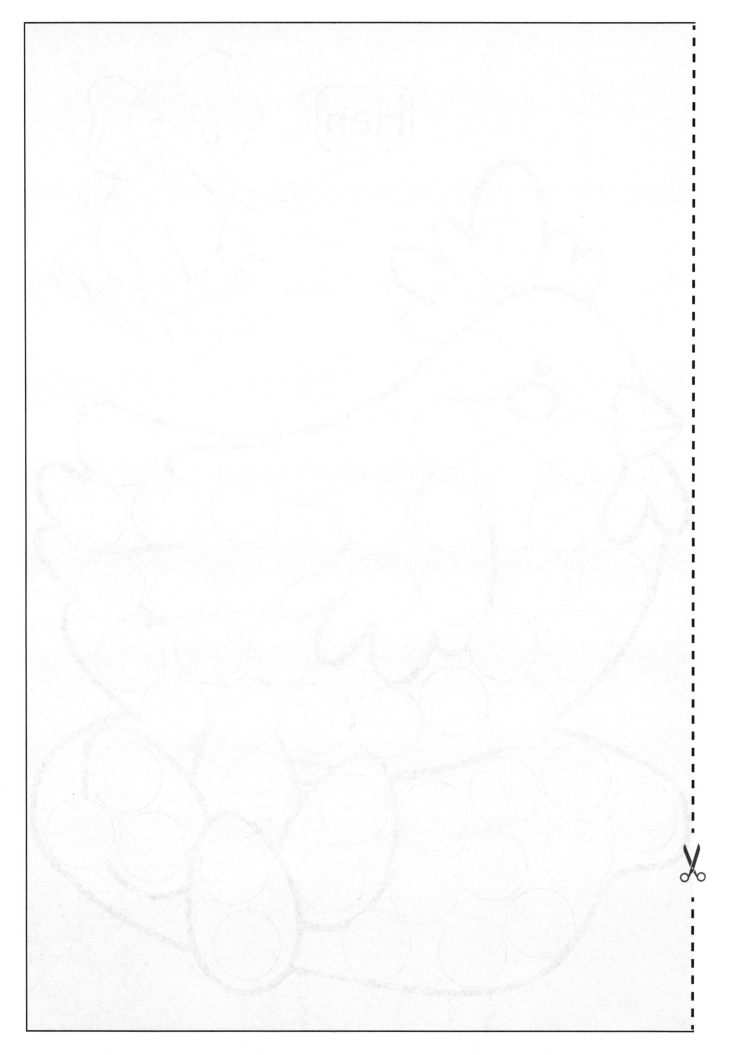

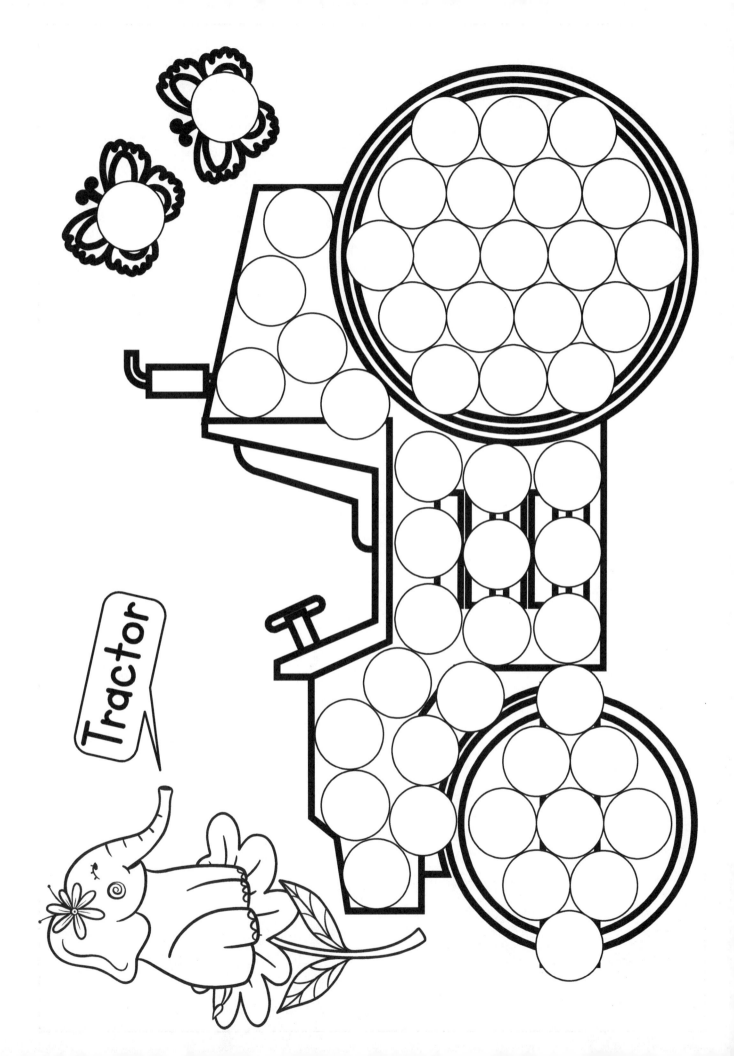

Tractor

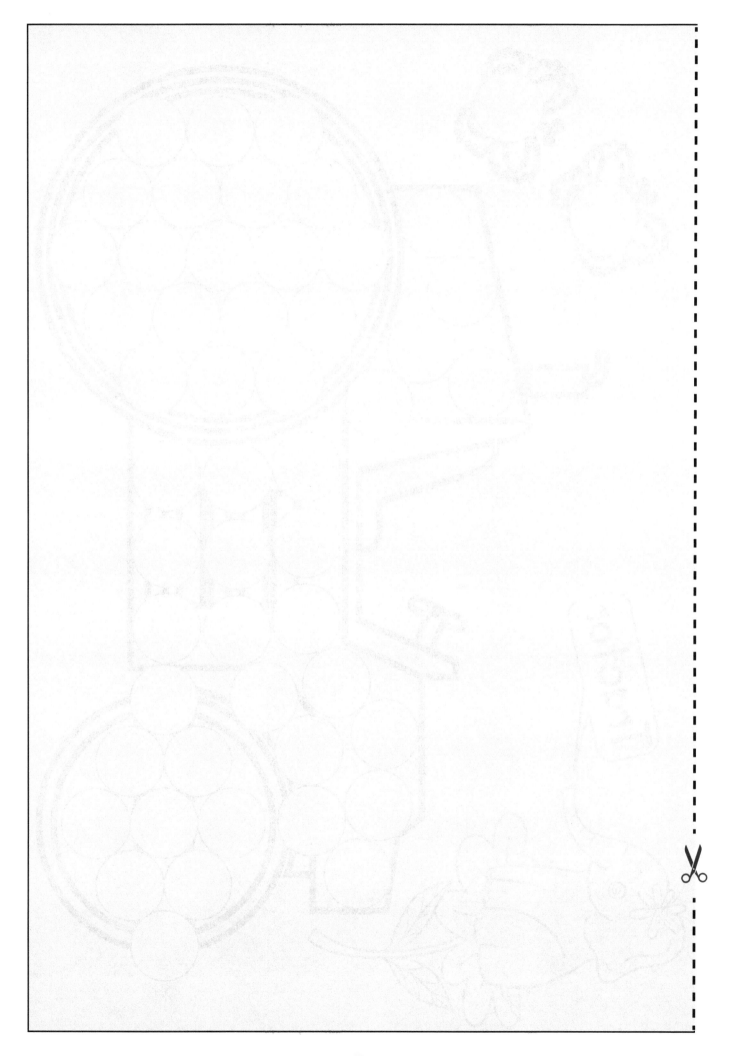

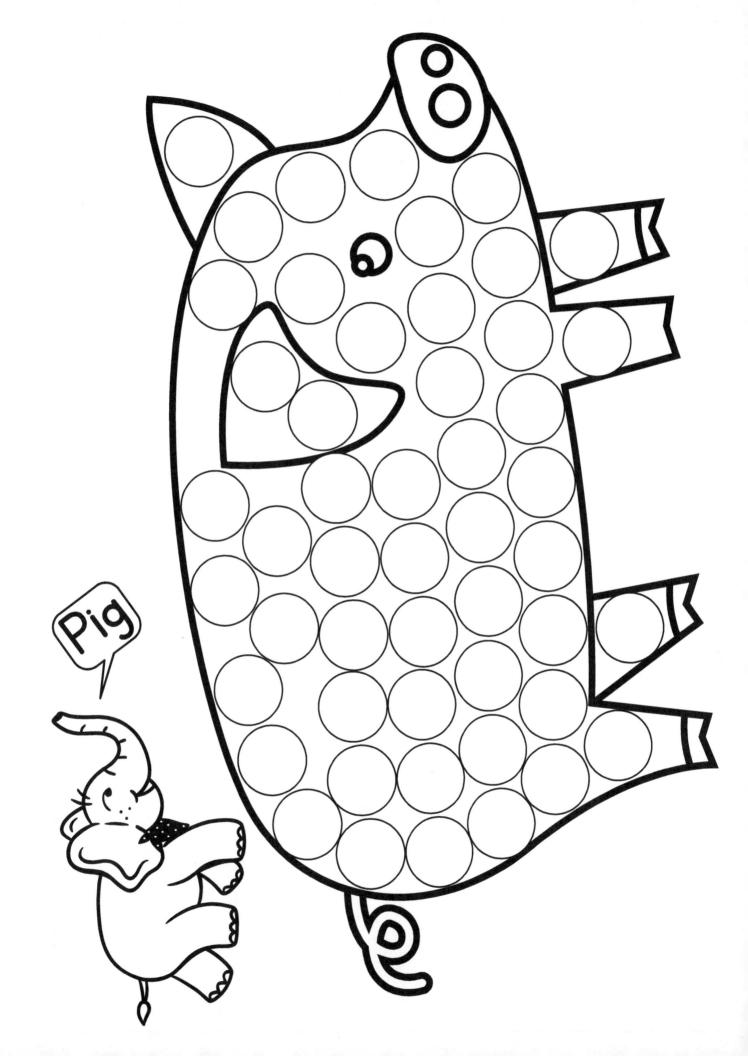

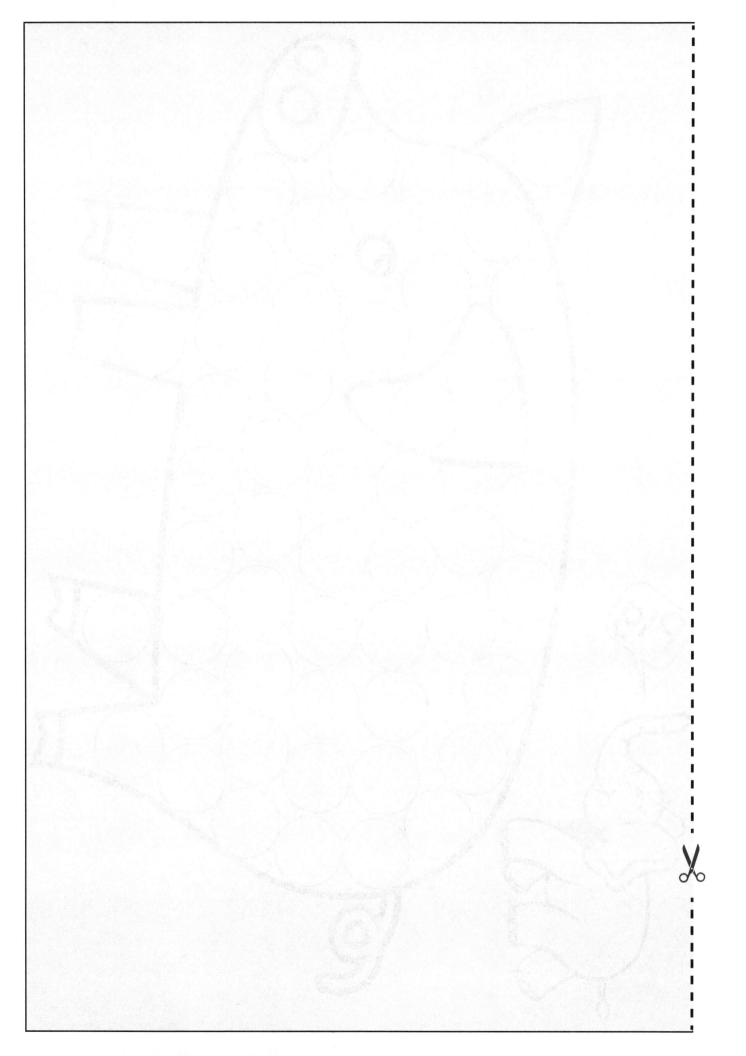

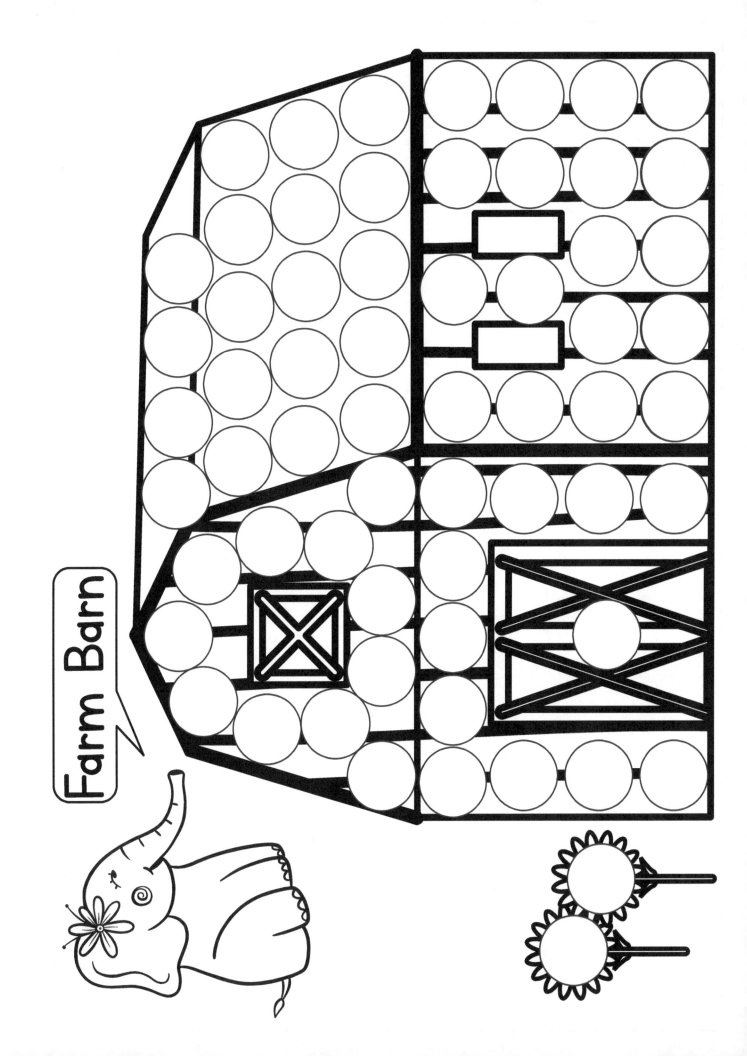

Farm Barn

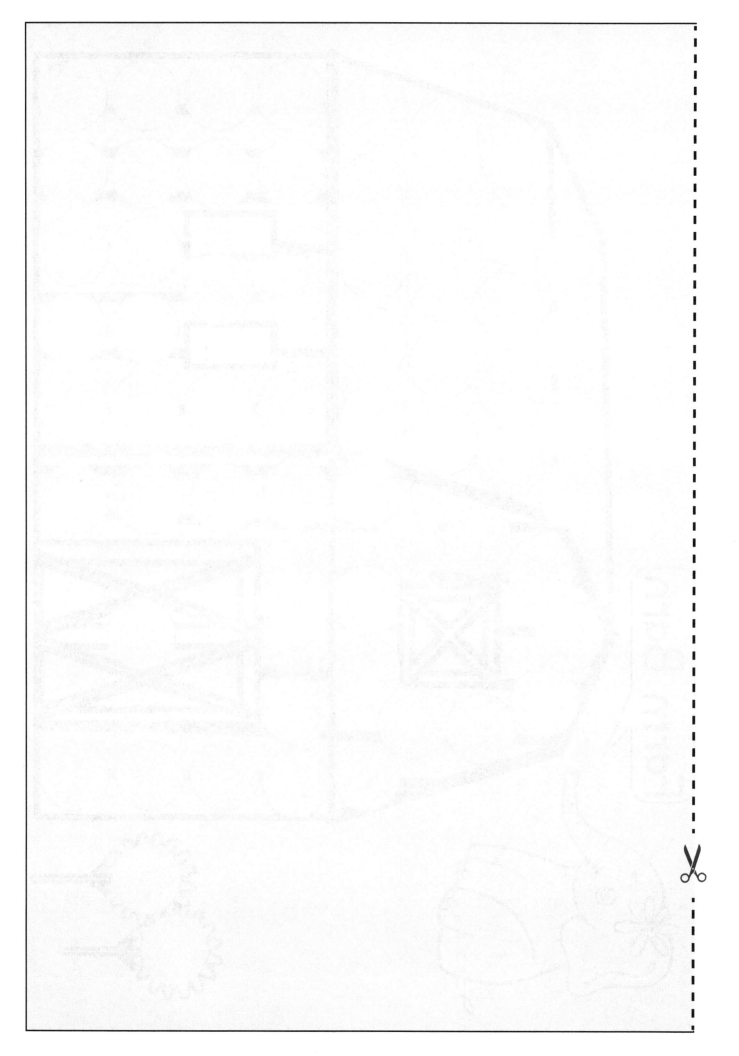

Have You Enjoyed This Book?

Scan the QR code below and let us know what you think. Include some pictures of your little ones' masterpieces. We'd love to see them!

Your review is really helpful to a small business like us.

United States

Thank you for your review!

If you purchased this book outside the United States you can make a review by scanning the QR codes below.

Canada   United Kingdom   Germany   Spain   Australia

Explore More Exciting Dot Markers Activity Books!

Scan the QR code below to discover all our books!

Vehicles	On The Farm	Dinosaurs	Christmas

  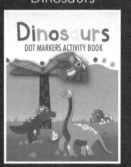 

If you live outside the United States you can purchase our books on Amazon in your country by scanning the QR codes below.

Canada	United Kingdom	Germany	Spain	Australia